Marriage

A Treasury of Words to Live By

Compiled by Robert B. Luce
Artwork by Kathy Orr

The C.R. Gibson Company
Norwalk, Connecticut
06856

Published by The C.R. Gibson Company, Norwalk, Connecticut 06856
Printed in the United States of America
ISBN 0-8378-2501-6
GB551

Introduction

From the dawn of the wedding day, through all the smiles and tears of the years to follow, marriage blossoms and is nurtured by a host of emotions, experiences and events.

This anthology of wisdom from those who have observed and lived through the many stages of marriage offers some words to live by and some wonderfully witty views from the heart. It is hoped this book will be an exciting look ahead for bride and groom and a happy reminder to all couples of all that is shared in married life.

The classic and elegant Victorian lace collages throughout are handcrafted by Kathy Orr.

Ed.

Husband and Wife

I will woo her, I will go with her into the wilderness
and comfort her: there I will restore her vineyards
turning The Vale of Trouble
into the Gate of Hope...
On that day she shall call me "My husband".

I will betroth to you myself forever,
betroth you in lawful wedlock
with unfailing devotion and love;
I will betroth to you myself
to have and to hold...

Hosea 2:14

Therefore shall a man leave his father and mother,
and shall cleave unto his wife:
and they shall be one flesh.

Genesis 2:24

Let marriage be held in honor among all...
Hebrews 13:4

O my heart's heart, and you who are to me
More than myself, God be with you
Keep you in strong obedience leal and true
To him whose noble service setteth free;
Make your joys many and your sorrows few,
Bless you in what you hear and what you do,
Yes, perfect you as he would have you be.

Christina Rossetti

Blessed are you, Holy One of the Earth,
who creates the fruit of the vine.
Blessed are you, Holy One of the Universe,
You have created all things for your Glory.
Blessed are you, Holy One of the World.
Through you mankind lives.
Blessed are you, Holy One of the World.
You made a man and woman in your image;
after your likeness, that they may perpetuate life.
Blessed are you, Holy One of All Nature,
who makes Zion rejoice with her children.
Blessed are you, Holy One of the Cosmos,
who makes the bride and bridegroom to rejoice.
Blessed are you, Holy One of All,
who created joy and gladness,
bride and bridegroom, mirth and song,
pleasure and delight, love, fellowship,
peace and friendship.

The Hebrew Seven Blessings

The time span of union is eternity.
This life is a jar, and in it the pure wine.
If we aren't together what use is the jar?

The moment I heard my first love story I began seeking you,
Not realizing the search was useless.
Lovers don't meet somewhere along the way,
They are in another's soul from the beginning.
You are the sea, I am the fish...

I am a crystal goblet in my love's hand
Look into my eyes if you don't believe me.

Persian Love Poem

Marriage hath in it less of beauty, but more of safety, than the single life; it hath more care, but less danger; it is more merry, and more sad; it is full of sorrows, and fuller of joys; it lies under more burdens, but it is supported by all the strengths of love, and charity, and those burdens are delightful.

Bishop Jeremy Taylor

God did not create woman from man's head, that he should command her, nor from his feet, that she should be his slave, but rather from his side, that she should be near his heart.

The Talmud

Marriage is a lottery in which men stake their liberty and women their happiness.

Madame De Rieux

Now you will feel no rain, for each of you
will be shelter to the other.
Now you will feel no cold, for each of you
will be warmth to the other.
Now there is no loneliness for you.
Now you are two persons, but there is only one life before you.

Go now to your dwelling place, to enter into the days
of your togetherness,
And may your days be good, and long together.

Apache prayer of benediction

Here's to matrimony, the high sea for which no compass has yet been invented.

Heinrich Heine

Togetherness

If ever two were one, then surely we.
If ever man were lov'd by wife, then thee;
If ever wife was happy in a man,
Compare with me ye women if you can.
I prize thy love more than whole Mines of gold,
Or all the riches that the East doth hold.
My love is such that Rivers cannot quench,
Nor ought but love from thee, give recompense.
Thy love is such I can no way repay,
The heavens reward thee manifold I pray.
Then while we live, in love let's so persevere,
That when we live no more, we may live ever.

Anne Bradstreet

There shall be such a oneness between you that
when one weeps, the other shall taste salt.

Proverb

Marriage resembles a pair of shears, so joined that they
cannot be separated; often moving in opposite directions,
yet always punishing anyone who comes between them.

Sydney Smith

In love the paradox occurs that two beings become one and yet remain two.

Erich Fromm

...for there is nothing greater and better than this — when a husband and wife keep a household in oneness of mind, a great woe to their enemies and joy to their friends, and win high renown.

Homer

There is no more lovely, friendly and charming relationship, communion or company than a good marriage.

Martin Luther

What greater thing is there for two human souls than to feel that they are joined... to strengthen each other... to be at one with each other in silent, unspeakable memories.

George Eliot

The Fountains mingle with the River
And the Rivers with the Ocean,
The winds of Heaven mix for ever
With a sweet emotion;
Nothing in the world is single;
All things by a law divine
In one spirit meet and mingle.
Why not I with thine?

Percy Bysshe Shelley

To get the full value of joy you must have
someone to divide it with.

Mark Twain

...he's more myself than I am. Whatever our souls are
made of, his and mine are the same... If all else perished
and he remained, I should still continue to be, and if all
else remained, and he were annihilated, the universe
would turn to a might stranger... He's always, always in
my mind; not as a pleasure to myself, but as my own
being.

Emily Bronte

But when two people are at one in their inmost hearts,
They shatter even the strength of iron and bronze.
And when two people understand each other in their
inmost hearts,
Their words are sweet and strong, like the fragrance of
orchids.

I Ching

...Love from one being to another can only be
that two solitudes come nearer, recognize and
protect and comfort each other.

Han Suyin

Independence

A good marriage is that in which each appoints the other guardian of his solitude.

Once the realization is accepted that even between the closest human beings infinite distances continue to exist, a wonderful living side by side can grow up, if they succeed in loving the distance between them which makes it possible for each to see the other whole against the sky.

Rainer Maria Rilke

Marriage is that relation between man and woman in which the independence is equal, the dependence mutual, and the obligation reciprocal.

Louis Kaufman Anspacher

You were born together, and together you shall be forevermore.
You shall be together when the white wings of death scatter your days.
Ay, you shall be together even in the silent memory of God.
But let there be spaces in your togetherness,
And let the winds of heaven dance between you.

Love one another, but make not a bond of love:
Let it rather be a moving sea between the shores of your souls.
Fill each other's cup but drink not from one cup.
Give one another of your bread but eat not from the same loaf.
Sing and dance together and be joyous,
but let each one of you be alone,
Even as the strings of a lute are alone
though they quiver with the same music.

Give your hearts, but not into each other's keeping.
For only the hand of Life can contain your hearts.
And stand together yet not too near together:
For the pillars of the temple stand apart,
And the oak tree and the cypress grow
not in each other's shadow.

Kahlil Gibran

The essence of a good marriage is respect for each other's
personality combined with that deep intimacy, physical,
mental, and spiritual, which makes a serious love between
man and woman the most fructifying of all human experi-
ences. Such love, like everything that is great and precious,
demands its own morality, and frequently entails a sacrifice
of the less to the greater; but such sacrifice must be volun-
tary, for, where it is not, it will destroy the very basis of the
love for the sake of which it is made.

Bertrand Russell

A good relationship has a pattern like a dance and is built on some of the same rules. The partners do not need to hold on tightly, because they move confidently in the same pattern, intricate but gay and swift and free, like a country dance of Mozart's. To touch heavily would be to arrest the pattern and freeze the movement, to check the endlessly changing beauty of its unfolding. There is no place here for the possessive clutch, the clinging arm, the heavy hand; only the barest touch in passing. Now arm in arm, now face to face, now back to back — it does not matter which. Because they know they are partners moving to the same rhythm, creating a pattern together, and being invisibly nourished by it.

Anne Morrow Lindbergh

Passion

Come live with me and be my love,
And we will all the pleasures prove
That hills and valleys, dales and fields
And all the craggy mountains yields.

There we will sit upon the rocks
And see the shepherds feed their flocks,
By shallow rivers to whose falls
Melodious birds sing madrigals.

And I will make thee beds of roses
With a thousand fragrant posies,
A cap of flowers and a kirtle
Embroidered all the leaves of myrtle.

A gown made of the finest wool
Which from our pretty lambs we pull;
Fair lined slippers for the cold,
With buckles of the purest gold;

A belt of straw and ivy buds,
With coral clasps and amber studs:
And if these pleasures may thee move,
Come live with me and be my love.

Christopher Marlowe

You, because you love me, hold
Fast to me, caress me, be
Quiet and kind, comfort me
With stillness, say nothing at all.
You, because I love you, I
Am strong from you. I uphold
You. The water is alive
Around us. Living water
Runs in the cut earth between
Us. You, my bride, your voice speaks
Over the water to me.
Your hands, your solemn arms,
Cross the water and hold me.
Your body is beautiful.
It speaks across the water.
Bride, sweeter than honey, glad
Of heart, our hearts beat across
The bridge of our arms. Our speech
Is speech of the joy in the night
Of gladness. Our words live.
Our words are children dancing
Forth from us like stars on water.
My bride, my well beloved,
Sweeter than honey, than ripe fruit,
Solemn, grave, a flying bird,
I love you. Be good to me.
I am strong for you. I uphold
You. The dawn of ten thousand
Dawns is afire in the sky.
The water flows in the earth.
The children laugh in the air.

Kenneth Rexroth

...because two bodies, naked and entwined,
leap over time, they are invulnerable,
nothing can touch them, they return to the source,
there is no you, no I, no tomorrow,
no yesterday, no names, the truth of two
in a single body, a single soul,
oh total being...

Octavio Paz

When you came, you were like red wine and honey,
And the taste of you burnt my mouth with its sweetness.
Now you are like morning bread,
Smooth and pleasant.
I hardly taste you at all, for I know your savor;
But I am completely nourished.

Amy Lowell

Many a man has fallen in love with a girl
in a light so dim he would not have chosen
a suit by it.

Maurice Chevalier

Give me a kiss, and to that a score;
Then to twenty, add a hundred more:
To make that thousand up a million, and when that's done.
Let's kiss afresh, as when first begun.

Hesperides to Anthea

The glances over cocktails
That seemed to be so sweet,
Don't seem quite so amorous
Over Shredded Wheat.

Anonymous

I hereby give myself. I love you. You are the only being whom I can love absolutely with my complete self, with all my flesh and mind and heart. You are my mate, my perfect partner, and I am yours. You must feel this now, as I do... It was a marvel that we ever met. It is some kind of divine luck that we are together now. We must never, never part again. We are, here in this, necessary beings, like gods. As we look at each other we verify, we know, the perfection of our love, we recognize each other. Here is my life, here if need be is my death.

Iris Murdoch

The sense of the world is short,–
Long and various the report,–
To love and be beloved:
Men and Gods have not outlearned it;
And how oft soe'er they've turned it,
'Tis not to be improved.

Ralph Waldo Emerson

Shall we roam, my love,
To the twilight grove

When the moon is rising bright?
Oh, I'll whisper there
In the cool night air,
What I dare not in broad daylight.

I'll tell thee a part
Of the thoughts that start
To being when thou art nigh
And thy beauty more bright
Than the stars soft light
Shall seem as a weft from the sky.
When the pale moonbeam
On tower and stream
Sheds a flood of silver sheen,
How I love to gaze
As the cold ray strays
O'er thy face, my heart's throned queen!

Wilt thou roam with me
To the restless sea
And linger upon the steep
And list to the flow
Of the waves below
How they toss and roar and leap?

Those boiling waves
And the storm that raves
At night o'er their foaming crest,

Resemble the strife,
That from earliest life,
The passions have waged in my breast.
Oh come then and rove
To the sea or the grove
When the moon is rising bright,
And I'll whisper there
In the cool night air
What I dare not in broad daylight.

Percy Bysshe Shelley

Disagreements

A happy marriage is the union of two good forgivers.

Robert Ouillen

What makes a marriage last is for a man and a woman to continue to have things to argue about.

Rex Stout

It is as hard for God to arrange a good marriage as it was for Him to divide the Red Sea.

Jewish Proverb

Often the difference between a successful marriage and a mediocre one consists of leaving about three or four things a day unsaid.

Harlan Miller

The test of a man or woman's breeding is how they behave in a quarrel.

George Bernard Shaw

Life is an adventure in forgiveness.

Norman Cousins

Anger in its time and place
May assume a kind of grace.
It must have some reason in it,
And not last beyond a minute.

Charles and Mary Lamb

The best part of married life is the fights.
The rest is merely so-so.

Thornton Wilder

Love is patient and kind; love is not jealous or boastful;
it is not arrogant or rude. Love does not insist on its
own way; it is not irritable or resentful...Love bears all
things, believes in all things, endures in all things.
Love never ends.

I Corinthians 13:4-8

If you want peace in your house, do as your wife wants.

African Proverb

To keep your marriage brimming
With love in the marriage cup,
Whenever you're wrong, admit it;
Whenever you're right, shut up.

Ogden Nash

Marriage is an edifice that must be
rebuilt every day.

Andre Maurois

Trouble is part of your life,
and if you don't share it,
you don't give the person who loves you
enough chance to love you enough.

Dinah Shore

I have learned that only two things are necessary to keep
one's wife happy. First, let her think she's having her way.
And second, let her have it.

Lyndon Baines Johnson

Marriage is one long conversation, chequered by disputes.

Robert Louis Stevenson

Be to her virtues very kind,
Be to her faults a little blind.

Matthew Prior

It is not marriage that fails; it is people that fail. All that
marriage does is to show people up.

Harry Emerson Fosdick

Let's contend no more, Love,
Strive nor weep:
All be as before, Love,
— Only sleep!

Robert Browning

Money

There are several ways in which to apportion the family income, all of them unsatisfactory.

Robert Benchley

Frugality is an enriching virtue; a virtue I never could acquire myself; but I was lucky to find it in a wife, who thereby became a fortune to me. With frugality there will be no lack; with extravagance, there is never enough.

Benjamin Franklin

There is only one thing for a man to do who is married to a woman who enjoys spending money, and that is to enjoy earning it.

E.W. Howe

Money cannot buy
The fuel of love
But it is excellent kindling.

W.H. Auden

...man's greatest wealth is to love on little with a contented mind, for a little is never lacking.

Lucretius

I choose the likely man in preference to the rich man. I want a man without money rather than money without a man. (Of two suitors for his daughter's hand).

Plutarch

If the husband gathers like bees, and the wife dispenses like the hour glass, they will get rich.

German Proverb

If you want a man's money, you should be willing to put up with his company.

John Cole McKim

If a man is wise, he gets rich, an' if he gets rich, he gets foolish or his wife does. That's what keeps the money movin' around.

Finley Peter Dunne

Because the cost of living is so high, it would be wise for many a young man to postpone marriage until she is earning more.

Anonymous

Let husband and wife infinitely avoid a curious distinction of mine and thine, for this hath caused all laws, and all suits, and all the wars in the world.

Jeremy Taylor

All heiresses are beautiful.

John Dryden

Love lives in a cottage or a castle.

Japanese Proverb

Children

It sometimes happens, even in the best of families, that a baby is born. This is not necessarily cause for alarm. The important thing is to keep your wits about you and borrow some money.

Elinor Goulding Smith

Who of us is mature enough for offspring before the offspring themselves arrive? The value of marriage is not that adults produce children but that children produce adults.

Peter De Vries

The first handshake in life is the greatest of all: the clasp of an infant fist around a parent's finger.

Mark Beltaire

Every child comes with the message that God is not yet discouraged of man.

Rabindranath Tagore

Better to be driven out from among men
than to be disliked of children.

R.H. Dana

In America there are two classes of travel —
first class and with children.

Robert Benchley

There never was a child so lovely
but his mother was glad to get him asleep.

Ralph Waldo Emerson

Before I got married I had six theories
about bringing up children;
now I have six children, and no theories.

Lord Rochester

Mothers give sons permission to be a prince
but the father must show him how...
Fathers give daughters permission to be
princesses. And mothers must show them
how. Otherwise, both boys and girls will grow
up and always see themselves as frogs.

Eric Berne

It is better to bind your children to you
by respect and gentleness than by fear.

Terence

The most important thing that parents can teach their children is how to get along without them.

Frank A. Clark

Your children are not your children.
They are the sons and daughters of life's longing for itself.
They come through you but are not from you,
And though they are with you yet they belong not to you.

You may give them your love but not your thoughts,
For they have their own thoughts.
You may house their bodies but not their souls,
For their souls dwell in the house of tomorrow
Which you cannot visit, not even in your dreams.

You may strive to be like them,
But seek not to make them like you.
For life goes not backwards nor tarries with yesterday.
You are the bows from which your children as living arrows
are set forth.

Kahlil Gibran

Advice to a young mother and father:
The days are long, but the years are short.

Anonymous

Children begin by loving their parents. After a time they judge them. Rarely, if ever, do they forgive them.

Oscar Wilde

Respect the child. Be not too much his parent.
Trespass not on his solitude.

Emerson

My mother had a great deal of trouble with me
but I think she enjoyed it.

Samuel Clemens

There are only two lasting bequests we can hope to give
our children. One of these is roots, the other wings.

Hodding Carter

Is this the little girl I carried?
Is this the little boy at play?
I don't remember growing older,
When did they?

When did she get to be a beauty?
When did he grow to be so tall?
Wasn't it yesterday
When they were small?

Sunrise, sunset, sunrise, sunset,
Swiftly flow the days.
Seedlings turn overnight to sunflowers,
Blossoming even as we gaze.

Sunrise, sunset, sunrise, sunset,

Swiftly fly the years.
One season following another.
Laden with happiness and tears.

Now is the little boy a bridegroom.
Now is the little girl a bride.
Under the canopy I see them,
Side by side.

Sheldon Harnick
Jerry Bock

Age

Love is what you've been through with somebody.

James Thurber

It is threads, hundreds of tiny threads, which sew people together through the years. That's what makes a marriage last — more than passion or sex.

Simone Signoret

Marriage is our last, best chance to grow up.

Reverend Joseph Barth

Come, let's be a comfortable couple and take care of each other! How glad we shall be, that we have somebody we are fond of always, to talk to and sit with.

Charles Dickens

The habit of living together soon gave rise to the finest feelings known as humanity, conjugal love and paternal affection.

Jen Jacques Rousseau

When a woman gets married it's like jumping into a hole in the ice in the middle of winter: you do it once, and you remember it the rest of your days.

Maxim Gorky

If the bullock and the cart keep together, what does it matter how many ups and downs there are?

Indian Proverb

A certain sort of talent is almost indispensable for people who would spend years together and not bore themselves to death… to dwell happily together, they should be versed in the niceties of the heart, and born with a faculty for willing compromise… should laugh over the same sort of jests and have many an old joke between them which time cannot wither nor custom stale…

Robert Louis Stevenson

The sum which two married people owe to one another defies calculation. It is infinite debt, which can only be discharged through all eternity.

Goethe

Immature love says: "I love you because I need you."
Mature love says: "I need you because I love you."

Erich Fromm

To love a person means to agree
to grow old with him.

Albert Camus

A happy marriage is a long conversation
that seems all too short.

Andre Maurois

Like everything which is not the involuntary
result of fleeting emotion, but the creation
of time and will, any marriage, happy or
unhappy, is infinitely more interesting and
significant than any romance,
however passionate.

W.H. Auden

When you are old and gray and full of sleep,
And nodding by the fire, take down this book,
And slowly read, and dream of the soft look
Your eyes had once, and of their shadows deep;

How many loved your moments of glad grace,
And loved your beauty with love false or true;
But one man loved the pilgrim soul in you,
And loved the sorrows of your changing face...

William Butler Yeats

My lizard, my lively writher,
May your limbs never wither,
May the eyes in your face
Survive the green ice
Of envy's mean gaze;
May you live out your life,
Without hate, without grief,
And your hair ever blaze,
In the sun, in the sun,
When I am undone,
When I am no one.

Theodore Roethke

Best trust the happy moments... The days that make us
happy make us wise.

John Masefield

If thou must love me, let it be for nought
Except for love's sake only. Do not say,
"I love her for her smile — her look — her way
Of speaking gently, — for a trick of thought
That falls in well with mine, and certes brought
A sense of pleasant ease on such a day"—
For these things in themselves, Beloved, may
Be changed, or change for thee, — and love, so wrought,
May be unwrought so. Neither love me for
Thine own dear pity's wiping my cheeks dry, —
A creature might forget to weep, who bore

Thy comfort long, and lose thy love thereby!
But love me for love's sake, that evermore
Thou mayest love on, through love's eternity.

Elizabeth Barrett Browning

May I look on you when my last hour comes; may I hold
you, as I sink, with my failing hand.

Albius Tibullis

To me, fair friend, you never can be old,
For as you when first your eye I ey'd,
Such seems your beauty still.

William Shakespeare

There is nothing false in thee.
In thy heat the youngest boy
Has warmth and light.
In thee the quills of the sun
Find adornment.
What does not die
Is with thee.

Thou art clothed in robes of music.
Thy voice awakens wings.

And still more with thee
Are the flowers of earth made bright.

Upon thy deeps the fiery sails
Of heaven glide.

Thou art the radiance and the joy.
Thy heart shall only fail
When all else has fallen.

What does not perish
Lives in thee.

Kenneth Patchen

Trust

It is absurd to say that a man can't love one woman all his life as it is to say that a violinist needs several violins to play the same piece of music.

Honore de Balzac

When the one man loves the one woman and the one woman loves the one man, the very angels leave heaven and come and sit in that house and sing for joy.

Brahma

Gentlemen, to the lady without whom I should never have survived for eighty, nor sixty, nor yet thirty years. Her smile has been my lyric, her understanding, the rhythm of the stanza. She has been the spring wherefrom I have drawn the power to write the words. She is the poem of my life.

Oliver Wendell Holmes

Those who love deeply never grow old; they may die of old age, but they die young.

Arthur Wing Pinero

A good husband makes a good wife.
Robert Burton

If I can't be who I am, who would I most like to be? Lady Churchill's second husband.
Winston Churchill

I believe that love cannot be bought except with love, and he who has a good wife wears heaven in his hat.
John Steinbeck

It is better to be faithful than famous.
Theodore Roosevelt

Marriage is popular because it combines the maximum of temptation with the maximum of opportunity.
George Bernard Shaw

To be married at least should be the one poetical act of a man's life. If you fail in this respect, in what respect will you succeed?
Henry David Thoreau

Nothing... is more beautiful than the love that has weathered the storms of life...
Jerome K. Jerome

ACKNOWLEDGMENTS

The editor and publisher have made every effort to trace the ownership of all copyrighted material and to secure permission from copyright holders of such material. In the event of any question arising to the use of any material, the publisher and editor, while expressing regret for inadvertent error, will be pleased to make any necessary corrections in future printings. Thanks are due the following authors, publishers, publications and agents for permission to use the material indicated.

Permission to quote George Bernard Shaw granted by The Society of Authors on behalf of the Bernard Shaw Estate.

From THE PROPHET by Kahlil Gibran Copyright © 1923 by Kahlil Gibran and renewed 1951 by Administrators C.T.A. of Kahlil Gibran Estate of Mary G. Gibran. Reprinted by Permission of Alfred A. Knopf, Inc.

Excerpt from THE BENCHLEY ROUNDUP by Robert Benchley. Copyright © 1954 by Nathaniel Benchley. Reprinted by permission of HarperCollins Publishers.

Excerpt from THE MATCHMAKER by Thornton Wilder. Copyright © 1955, 1957 by Thornton Wilder. Reprinted by permission of HarperCollins Publishers.

Excerpt from THE ART OF LOVING by Erich Fromm. Copyright © 1956 by Erich Fromm. Reprinted by permission of HarperCollins Publishers.

From THE BOOK AND THE BROTHERHOOD by Iris Murdoch. Copyright © 1987 by Iris Murdoch. Used by Permission of Viking Penguin, a division of Penguin Books USA Inc.

SUNRISE, SUNSET—Sheldon Harnick, Jerry Bock © 1964—ALLEY MUSIC CORP. & TRIO MUSIC CO., INC. Used by Permission. All rights reserved.

THE COMPLETE POETICAL WORKS OF AMY LOWELL. Copyright © renewed 1983 by Houghton Mifflin Company, Brinton P. Roberts, and G. D'Andelot Belin, Esquire. Reprinted by permission of Houghton Mifflin Company. All rights reserved.

The following reprinted by permission of New Directions Publishing Corporation: Octavio Paz: The Collected Poems of Octavio Paz, 1957-1987. Copyright © 1972, 1986 by Octavio Paz and Eliot Weinberger. Kenneth Rexroth: Collected Shorter Poems of Kenneth Rexroth. Copyright © 1952 by Kenneth Rexroth. Kenneth Patchen: Collected Poems of Kenneth Patchen. Copyright © 1942 by Kenneth Patchen.

Excerpt from THE COMPLETE BOOK OF ABSOLUTELY PERFECT BABY AND CHILD CARE by Elinor Goulding Smith Copyright © 1957 by Joseph and Daniel Smith.

MARRIAGE & MORALS by Bertrand Russell Copyright © Routledge London, England.

"Wish for a Young Wife," copyright © 1963 by Beatrice Roethke, admistratix of the Theodore Roethke. From THE COLLECTED POEMS OF THEODORE ROETHKE by Theodore Roethke. Used by permission of Doubleday, a division of Bantam Doubleday Dell Publishing Group, Inc.

From WITHOUT A STITCH IN TIME by Peter DeVries. Copyright 1943, 1946, 1947, 1948, 1949, 1950, 1951, 1952, 1953, 1954, © 1956, 1959, 1961, 1962, 1963, 1964, 1968, 1969, 1970, 1971, 1972 by Peter DeVries. By permission of Little Brown and Company.